SOLIDARITY WITH THE FLESH EATING MOSAIC AND OTHER POEMS

For Sashi

SOLIDARITY WITH THE FLESH EATING MOSAIC AND OTHER POEMS

by

RAJ DRONAMRAJU

© 2011 Raj Dronamraju

All rights reserved. No part of this book may be reproduced in any form or by any means, electronic or mechanical, including photocopying, recording, or by any information storage or retrieval system, without written permission.

Post Egoism Media
www.postegoism.net

ISBN: 978-0-578-08502-9

CONTENTS

INTRODUCTION   11
BIOGRAPHY   13

PART I

OTHER GODS   17
MICHAEL'S SOMERSAULT   19
SOLIDARITY WITH THE FLESH EATING MOSAIC   20
I'LL MARRY THE NURSE   21
THE DRACULA REFERENCE THAT NEED NOT APPLY   22
DELICIOUS AGONY   23
AGENTS OF DELIBERATE MISERY   24
REFERRING TO ORIGAMI   25
THE DISHONESTY BROTHERS   26
HEY LOCAL MACHINE   27
EVENING INTERRUPTUS   28
THE MILLION DOLLAR QUARTET   29

THE VACUUM ABHORRED BY NATURE TRIUMPHS	30
1984 NEVER HAPPENED	31
A SIMULTANEOUS SCHEREZADE	32
THERE'S MURDER IN A WHORE'S LAST BREATH	33
THE THIRD CONUNDRUM	34
AGGRESSIVELY THE SUN	35
DEVIL HANDED SAMUEL	36
AMBULANCE	37
DARK MONK FREAKOUT	38
A CRUEL REMINDER	39
THE GRAPEFRUIT THEOREM	40
DUALITY PROCESSIONS	41
MADWOMAN	42
CHILDREN'S BOOK AUTHOR	43
KNUCKLEFRUIT	44
LURKING	45
NEEDLENOSE PLIERS	46
GIRL TALKING TO MIDNIGHT	47

PART II

OUR INTREPID REPORTER	51
THE ELEPHANT SYMBOL	52
THE WORLD IS A RUIN	53
ANGEL IN THE DARK	54
THE PSYCHEDELIA OF CHILDREN	55
DEVICE FOR FLIRTATION	56
I KILLED A DRIFTER	57
PHAROAH COMPARISONS	58
FOR ST	59
ON READING OSWALD SPENGLER FOR THE FIRST TIME	60
NO NEED TO BUY APPLES	61
PLANET SEXY	62
I WANT TO BE ON GOOD TERMS	63
CHILD MOLESTER SANTA'S	64
14x50	65
THE RITUAL OF BEING INSIDE	66
THE LOVE THAT WILL KILL YOU	67
LIKE A HUSBAND FROM THE LOWER CLASSES	68

A FRIEND OF BEAUTY	69
THE TRUTH WILL HARM YOU	70
THE ORPHANS	71
HEAVY LEGS	72
MIDNIGHT AT THE WAX MUSUEM	73
DIVINE LIFE ORGANIZATION	74
HUMPTY DUMPTY BETRAYAL	75
FRIENDS OF YOUR OWN AGE	76
MONEYSTOMACH	77
FIVE DIFFERENT TYPES OF FREE EXPRESSION FIGHTING TO BE FIRST THROUGH THE EXIT	78
THE COLDEST DAY OF THE YEAR	79
THE PEOPLE WHO KNOW DEATH	80

INTRODUCTION

Experience is the currency we barter and exchange for the inspiration in which to write both poetry and prose.

Experience is defined by the requisite amount (different in each person's case) of knowledge gathered through actual hands-on exposure rather than second hand knowledge.

For a lot of people, experience is like the bullets bouncing off Superman's chest not leaving any permanent damage but also not imparting any new wisdom.

For those of us who want something more, we look for art that will swallow our minds whole and that leaves no room for daylight from the outside world.

We look for art that changes us by both relating to experiences we've had previously and opening up our minds by introducing new ideas.

The end result is our complexity as human beings and something else which is understanding.

Our understanding of the world is likely to be different than the understanding of the world of the person standing next to us.

We gather baggage on this trip of experience/understanding/knowledge as well but hopefully not enough that it weighs us down and prevents future trips.

After all, there is not an age in which the ability to absorb something from a new experience ceases to exist.

Words give voice to our perspective filtered through our personality.

The process in which these words are put into a semblance of sense….
This is called poetry!

BIOGRAPHY

Raj Dronamraju notices that people often describe themselves through their work. He has worked for a breast implant manufacturer, a dental implant manufacturer, and a company that manufactures sonar apparatus for submarines. He is the author of a six volume semi-autobiographical series of novels and another book of poetry, *The Return of the Magnificent Ninny and Other Poems*. Raj Dronamraju is an American but currently lives in Malaysia and teaches English at a local university.

PART I

OTHER GODS

When the lie that comes from deep within us
Stretches out to the close quartered boundaries of our tiny comfort zone
You hold it like a blanket covering the head in a leaky house
That's not a rainstorm that that's going to let up

Recognizing that morality is not so clearly defined
Despite the self-assurance of those who define it
Control is the similarity between all man-made dogma
From this Sunday onwards, I'll be sleeping in

And if hurting other people is the benchmark of good versus evil
Everything else is none of anybody's business
I'll sacrifice the superstitious me in the privacy of my own home
My rituals are private, personal, and elusive

It is noticed that saving other people's souls often produces mountains of
    corpses
Society forces you to prostrate before dogma five or more times a day
I'd rather be a hermit with no contact to the outside world
When religion and society mix, there's no room for freedom

When I'm happier with a mind as empty as Halloween
Stick a candle in my head and watch my eyes light up
That's not something that should be messed with
These small miracles are ethereal and life-affirming

And when I finally started living in public
Big, clumsy, loud, spastic
I smashed all the China in the shop
Until I figured out how to walk and talk on my own

Coming out the other end of below the waist faith,
I see there's pleasure in carnality unleashed
Comfort taken in illicit sex and other taboo pleasures
A conversion from this point on to the worshipping of….
Other Gods!

MICHAEL'S SOMERSAULT

He played the part of my mother at the theatre in practice
"Why don't you know how to tie your own shoes?"
This gambit has been discovered and shot down

He played the part of the dancer in my one happy memory
Don't get too close when he executes a flip
No need to worry that privilege will ever befriend or rub off on you

He played the part of the silent, sinister driver early Saturday morning
Nothing is left from Friday but bullseye pain dead center between the
        eyebrows
The grave has been dug….Let him wiggle his way out of this one

SOLIDARITY WITH THE FLESH EATING MOSAIC

Burning down the temple of Goth
Experience counts for almost nothing
She talked of experience
As she handed out candy and alcohol
This was the pep talk for those going in
To add to the high minded heroism

Cave Team Leader #1 was never seen again
Cave Team Leader #2 rolled away the stone
Cave Team Leader #3 tried to understand local dialects
Cave Team Leader #4 put a down payment on a house
Cave Team Leader #5 worked on becoming a much better person
Cave Team Leader #6 was just messing with you

These spelunkers grew up with patterns and bursts of light
They don't feel trapped by a locality
They feel no pressing need for any sort of change
Underground, aboveground, makes no difference to a happy man

One with the consumer of all living things
That moves too slowly to be pierced by the human eye
Not appearing as terrible to the servants of the great growing blue patch
It's fungal in nature, all horror fiction and conformity

I'LL MARRY THE NURSE

The hand of friendship was offered
The hand of friendship was slapped away
The trajectory of the spurned

In a drugstore rant,
I see no future in a brief moment's temper
And I wonder how I'm going get through the next 20 or 30 years

When I'm old and sick and you leave me on my own
And in the care of others so you can enjoy your good health
I'll make do with what I have
And I'll marry the nurse

I've always wanted to exclaim
With outrage on my side
"This time you've gone too far!"
Instead I'll make new friends
Invite myself to new social situations
And I'll marry the nurse

THE DRACULA REFERENCE
THAT NEED NOT APPLY

You are a house with many rooms
And in these rooms empty tables
And beds not slept in
The question of how to be comfortable with less

All the mirrors in the rooms
Have old newspapers taped over their surface
Like a vampire or werewolf stands self-conscious in front of them

Come and knock on the door
That's the conventional approach and will get you nowhere
Come and knock on the wall
Feel around for a secret passage

The house hides many from dawn until dusk
The night creatures come out and prowl around your superficiality
Worrying for nothing, you never went outside
The neighbors all know you as the ghost that haunts this house

DELICIOUS AGONY

O delicious agony
That shapes you in the wrong way

O closure driven consciousness
That seeks resolution for all parties
But accomplishes nothing

Childhood dream ogres
Step in to the present day
Elbowing you in the ribs, messing up your hair
When you least expect it
In the elevator, in the office

O the pain you can't live without
The self-created torturer's appointment is for life
Like little boys living in bombed out buildings
Wondering when their luck is going to change

AGENTS OF DELIBERATE MISERY

She helps herself to your bad dreams
It first appears to be an unobtrusive dysfunction
The national need for nightmare
The conjuring up of drama out of a situation that doesn't seem that bad

Do you dare to speak your mind?
Selected not elected
My life is overblown, too much attention focused inwards
Pain doesn't make you feel anymore alive because the pain is artificial and
      manufactured

They might have loved someone before you
But the necessary treatment was administered in time
She makes the cuts along her arm with symmetrical precision
The razor used is the negativity she harvests from knowing you

REFERRING TO ORIGAMI

And they folded emotions
Like origami
Into stiff bird shapes
Then they playacted the flight of the restrained

They kept the windows shut
Near a place where tigers go to die
The transformation of a man with skin of golden hue
Into a man with skin dripping with disgusting black goo
From the heavens to the pits - that's the journey backwards!

And they put the world on notice
That it could become part of a revolving mobile
Under threat of being hung up like windchimes
Origami prisoners suspended for display

THE DISHONESTY BROTHERS

How do you tell the criminals from your neighbors?
Your co-workers? From those that handle your groceries and your mail?
If the years that have passed have made our friendship an anachronism
We still share a mutual distrust of everything

In a condominium of contrasts
We waited for newspapers to bring on cynicism
And age to bring on feelings of weariness
And a time machine to reclaim our shared thrill in a day's random nonsense

And it is my plan to incorporate every difficulty I have ever had
Into an oath seldom used
Condemning others for all eternity
An eternity wherein you must tell the same joke over and over again
"A man is pulled over for speeding the second day in a row"
"There is a pig in the front passenger seat of his car"
"I thought I told you to take that pig to a zoo"
"I did and today I am taking him to the movies"

HEY LOCAL MACHINE

Hey Local Machine!
I don't think you can afford not to look outside
Bury the hatchet with gauche friends
That's how a revolution begins

There's a crack in the orderly linoleum living arrangement
All of the molecules bored to death
From the community to the nation and beyond

The hours you and I must work
Would quiet the song of a nightingale
Its lovely renditions for wide awake youth at late night hours

Pinpointing the sympathy factor
Feeling sorrow for one's autobiography
That's how a revolution begins

EVENING INTERRUPTUS

Voices raised in the street outside my house
An argument, more than an argument
The four letter words are pulled from their holster

I wonder why these two people, a man and a woman, were arguing
And what brought them to strife
And what made them so angry as to forget themselves in a public situation

The intense anger of the personal
Stains the day to day familiar contempt
Brings alive long submerged frustrations
"For a second, I hoped for your death"

And the conflict between two people, a man and a woman, makes them real
    in the eyes of the world
And what do I have to offer the world?
Musings in a battered notebook
Mindless hustle for three square meals a day

THE MILLION DOLLAR QUARTET

With sprigs of holly for the dunderheads to kiss under
And a serenade from little birds singing "we are superfluous"
Rows of genuflecting idolaters blinded by the sun
Physically kept on the other side of the partition by the bodyguards

The information age circus trap girls as companion
Serving two purposes for the million dollar quartet

Parasols ablaze and hurled at moving vehicles
Their protest is for show only
Nobody is taking them too seriously

"I can't be seen on the cover of your magazine"
The penile envy military complication as companion
Providing a buffer between the common people and the million dollar
      quartet

Lost and vulnerable
Tarot cards showing death and the fool

Pathetic used and empty
Refrigerated trucks bringing perishable items overland
For tonight's celebration of the wealthy

THE VACUUM ABHORRED BY NATURE TRIUMPHS

He made love to an air conditioned woman
An over rehearsed, over prepared argonaut journeying nowhere
Control! Mongoloid dreams of the spaceship mother

"You're a heartless swine" she pushes sound
As he reflects on being led for a lifetime
Control! The obligations of daytime….stars and planets call your name

The race that bred itself out of existence
By eliminating the gene called initiative
Control! I need your paralysis in order to build the perfect nation-state

1984 NEVER HAPPENED

The ranting and raving of a hysteric
Were taken as a serious warning by mole people
The types whose minds never see the light of day
There have been times we have had to make do with less
But there have been many times we had too much
Over consumption of a diet of rubbish has made the West fat, weak,
      incurious

No one's going to take you to room 101
Unless it's to show you a preview of the new television season
Remember rats spelled backwards is star
The telescreen has wi-fi and is user friendly for Tivo
Peace through strength, 24 hour cable
Total control over every thought/action or to gorge oneself on everything
The totalitarians chose the latter

A SIMULTANEOUS SCHEHERAZADE

All of the stories were downloaded at one time
Dreams like premonitions full of wild narratives and people we would see
    again
The human mind stretched to the breaking point

Scheherazade - coerced by the threat of murder
To disable the filters blocking the imagination
Too much, I won't remember a thing
In the years that have passed since we assigned an importance to
    entertainment
Our minds have not developed at the same speed

Every escape your cowardly soul could have ever wanted
Is but a click or keystroke away
The expressions of creativity bleed into one another
Making things up, now there are millions doing the same
There is no escape from escapism

THERE'S MURDER IN
A WHORE'S LAST BREATH

There's a terror train ride in the future of a casting couch girl
There's an anger shot widely missing the mark in the future of everybody's
        girl
A sunshine temperament denied
Becomes a supernova 50 times wide

I can't stomach any of this
There's murder in a whore's last breath
The injustice she feels can only be expressed as a strangled sob

I can't stomach any of this
Witness to the life of a whore
What brought her to this point
And the anger that had all but eaten her up inside

But oh how you'll toss and turn tonight
And oh you won't find sleep no matter where you look
And oh tomorrow how soiled and old you will feel

THE THIRD CONUNDRUM

Let the heart grow unimpressed
With what is small and entwined
For the ages with an immovable, granite mind
We have seen this twice before
You were first to recognize and call "head's up"
And no one thanks you

Preferring to leave it as a mystery
For the daily commuters on the pinhead express
An engorged right side
Your sweet smile saves you from those asking questions
I know the type, always equipped with a clipboard
And the desire to cross out names

Much harm to be done under the guise of fake kindness
You never cared for those things before
Women and children and the poor
Everyone should own one!

AGGRESSIVELY THE SUN

Aggressively the sun
Tore the night sky to bits
Ignoring its passive whimpering
Its barely audible protestations

Aggressively the sun
Prodded and manipulated the day's sweaty girth
Pushing it the full 360 degrees
Slapping it all the way

We fabricate our lives
In the delusion that this is nature
We are buffeted and rocked
By the real nature that cannot be stopped

Aggressively, I
Took our lives down a rocky path
I know no other way to conquer this existence

DEVIL-HANDED SAMUEL

Never make a deal
With a man standing behind your house
That you have not seen before
But who knows everything about you

Or

The one who rides through the night
With headlights turned off
You think he's doing you a favor
But one day you'll get the bill

For rhyme and reason's sake
There's a soul but I'm not sure where it's hidden

I'll fight life
For just a taste of self-respect
Iron-voiced Nazis in power positions
Won't cause me to make a worse mistake
By driving me to sign a contract with my oneness's worst enemy
My lone and rising oneness….Focus on getting above it all!!!

AMBULANCE

Today the elevators are not working
And there's more traffic than usual
Leading to more traffic jams
Especially when there's a minor fender bender
And the looky loos all stop and stare

I wasn't around during the carnage and the spectacle
You had given generously
To ladies with binoculars and nothing else to do
There was a boy at my high school
Who flipped his jeep over three days before his 18th birthday
His death was literal

When I heard about you, I couldn't raise the energy to leave the house
Centipede legs not in coordination
In a prone position, lazy and disloyal on the couch
I had no words to offer….just sounds
Hhhhhnnnnnmmmmmm
It was as if my tongue had been cut out

Hardened nipples, bugged out eyes
Today the Internet is down and there's no running water
One brave soldier felt around and
Found an excuse to his liking
Last night he went out with friends and
Partied like a Viking

This is your needy sickness
And how getting attention makes you feel better about yourself
When the lights flash and the siren wails and
The cars pull off to the side of the road
At least, people will have something to stare at

DARK MONK FREAKOUT

On second thought, don't bring it on
That's an appointment I don't plan on keeping
No ego, no worship, no courage
Nothing but the rawest survival stratagem
When you fall prey to a bad idea, it is like that

With enemies like this, you don't need friends
To pat you on the insecurity and push you into weakness
Put a lot of distance between that decade I and this decade I
To that decade I, me communicate a message
Perfect situation, you don't exist!
Blindfolded, faith eagerly steps off the ledge

Unhappy girls, we drew the curtain
Still you maintain a wax fruit life
Pale ghosts like empty vacuum cleaner bags
Waiting to suck up all the dirt and dust from
The floors of rooms made filthy by squalid humanity

Solitude is the happiest condition
But only if you have half a brain in your head

A CRUEL REMINDER

When February arrives, it catches us unprepared for mourning
Just like tornado season comes upon Kansas and Oklahoma each year
We know the date which brings us pain
And internally try to deal with it
However, imagination is a cruel, untamable beast
That cannot be saddled or caged or controlled by a loving heart or caring mind

"He would have been two" you say
I expect something like this but it still slaps and stings like cold water in the face
You expect nothing from me
I was all blank face and stoic strength when it happened
And said "Well it's just a lump of tissue to me"
Because I thought of it not yet as a human being
However when I saw the body
That at six months was remarkably fully formed
I was no longer so sure

This boy unnamed, unclaimed, and not spoken of
Expelled too early into this harsh world
Still born, I know he still lives every time I see that you are quiet and sad

THE GRAPEFRUIT THEOREM

Summing up my civilized mind
With a belligerent trigonometry
We are lines that do not stop
Sharp angles, unhesitatingly swinging
When we go parallel….It makes you feel threatened

What do you want to know that you currently do not know?
Numbers are omnipresent but grapefruits are magic
They are not mutually exclusive

I am a friend to knowledge
Won't go with my gut if my gut can't repeat back a summary of chapters 1
      through 5

DUALITY PROCESSIONS

He was the seducer and the seduced, he was the burden and the one strong enough to lift it, he was owner and renter, he was deeply involved and long past caring, he was pilot and passenger, he was burning brightly and the flame that went out

It was an honest mistake
It was desperation well hidden
Dragging my feet before attempting the procedure
It won't lead to marks or permanent disfigurement

It was an honest mistake
Plenty of guts still no glory
In the court of the ruthless monarch
I am denied the chance to present my case

MADWOMAN

Her 19th century words
"It's like being in jail"
Her 20th century curse
"I can't lower myself to feel happiness"
Stroking his carcass, at the beck and call
When they identify the ritual sacrifice, it will be the family

Ta-da, I must have my freedom
And all plotlines summarized
Mouthing the word "selfish"
When confronted with a choice of career over people
She is neither radiant nor well-loved
She is neither respected nor glamorized
When she is imitated, it will only bring doom upon the imitator

CHILDREN'S BOOK AUTHOR

I'm for raw reality
Revealed to the very young

The little train that couldn't
The small animal that was killed and eaten by hunters
The young boy who misbehaved and was never seen again

Life is hard and painful
Better get used to it
No one's going to magically appear to help you
Better get used to it
This is no fairy tale
Better get used to it
There are no happy endings
Better get used to it

KNUCKLEFRUIT

From whence you did your duty for 30 years
And were subsequently barred entrance to the palace of physical pleasure
Fell under the spell of a traveling necromancer
The black arts are only black because society deems them as so

They want to get their hands on the knucklefruit
She wants to cry out with the full force of released passion
Spent passion is a feeling worth holding on to
Hold on to well-being, happiness, lower blood pressure

Where were you yesterday afternoon?
We tried to reach you by phone
And also knocked on your door
That's a risky little inference in the corner of an eye
And the wet dispatch of a recent connection to living

They have gotten their hands on the knucklefruit
What goes in inside is our little secret
What goes on outside as the details emerge
Dirty little hands clinging to unhealthy substitutes
While we lay back in the aftermath of a mini-explosion

Open the gates, matchless one!
Both parties satisfied
Nothing exists except this room and the bed within

LURKING

Don't let me catch you
Under my feet or in the air above
I know you're watching me from behind the last tree
Surely, I can't fascinate you that much

Life story in a handkerchief
That you regularly put up to your nose
I am your vision of a peculiar, original state

But you see I am the product of rootless chaos
An existence not firmly planted on Terra Firma
Lack of security on a dailyweeklymonthly basis
I found out there was no safety net and now here I am

I wouldn't wish my life on a stillborn pig
Don't go trying to romanticize what I found excruciating

Don't let me catch you
Hiding in the bushes or following from a distance
I will be forced to sic a dog upon you
I will be forced to seek a restraining order

Passing nimbly through your own hollow days
Your fond worship of my wretchedness deeply frustrates me

NEEDLENOSE PLIERS

There's not enough custard for everyone
The portions are not equally distributed
He has more custard than me
No, I will not eat my custard quietly
Keeping the pressure on

She lies constantly
She does not deal with situations fairly and impartiality
She does not tell me what she tells other people
She plays both sides off against the middle
No, I will not overlook this behavior
Keeping the pressure on

Madmen, Madmen, Madmen
There is one madman even madder than before
Chips cashed in at midnight on April Fool's Day
Dreams that taste like dirt in the mouths of the populace
No, I won't let them explain this away with pie charts and bell graphs
Keeping the pressure on

GIRL TALKING TO MIDNIGHT

How do I get home afterwards?
My blindness took me far but not home afterwards
My naivety in the ways of others booked me first class passage

Figure in a cloak of darkness is a good listener
The door in the garage connects with the rest of the house bypassing
    sleeping elders
Figure in a cloak of darkness passes out advice

Perchance she doesn't turn onto the victim route
We drag who we are with us forever
The delicately instructed dirtied up dolls
Have big, powerful, red hands that can crush aluminum cans

Perchance she doesn't stop for victimhood
The best and brightest live in a summer of one million years
The rest are in states of dull inertia jumping occasionally when shocked by
    memory jolts like electricity

PART II

OUR INTREPID REPORTER

Better put some ice on that….it's going to swell
You did something, made a decision, acted on it
I'm only watching, taking notes
Speak directly into the microphone
How do you spell your name?

Love's so easily trampled during a crowd's blind panic
Cue the impersonator and the one who can recognize this and deliver the
    critique
Recording the facts for consumption by a faceless audience
Under a byline no one would ever be proud of

I will remain aware in the marketplace of ideas
Not purchasing anything, only window shopping
Seeking ways to personalize the story
Bringing it down to the level of human interest

I wouldn't say any of this if I didn't have proof
Carefully footnoted references
Truckloads of trivia arriving on the hour

Wagging a finger of correction
At conversationalists who will never converse here again
How rude, how rude
To stand to be corrected by a twerp

THE ELEPHANT SYMBOL

High up in the treetops
Where the laughing people go
To escape their daily scolding

We all know something of dreams and an unforgiving reality
And the inability to tell the difference
This the pachyderm does not forget
Along with being driven away by firecrackers from a potential food source
Or forced to stand on two legs and wear a dress

High up off the ground
Where an afternoon's stillness is like music
I can breathe and stretch to the full boundaries of me
The pachyderm that means so much
Strength, fertility, creator, this world and cycle
Is prodded with sticks when it wants to do something on its own
How disappointed I was
To be prodded with sticks
When I tried to go in a different direction from the rest of the herd

THE WORLD IS A RUIN

The world is a ruin
And it's beautiful

Valleys and canyons scooped out
Pockmarked like the face of a pimply adolescent

Oceans undulating and overflowing
Like beverages borne on the tray of an unsteady waitress

Mountains jutting upwards
Colossal blemishes
Disrupting the even flow of the topography

Scars upon the planet
Beauty marks of creation
I love each geographical, geological, seismic imperfection
Is this where we talk about volcanoes?

THE ANGEL IN THE DARK

The smell of a rented room
The taste and texture of well-worn sheets
The careless, faded lives that padded around in here before you

Now you try to find one to pin your hopes on
This cavern's not so easily found
Not so easily seen from the road or the cliff

Apparently, I and all play coy games
Don't have the power of recognition
Could never quite grasp this self-imposed isolation

A spell woven by a wizard
A crusader from out of dreams
Fantastic but the dark doesn't move

In a rented room
You push something too heavy to be moved
And resort to fantasy for something better

THE PSYCHEDELIA OF CHILDREN

"Mr. Octopus lives in the sky"
My wife's nephew explains to me
"ON MARS"
He adds for emphasis

I connect and I see
As you go off on your dream
My trip is sometimes backward to childhood
Where logical connectors are not needed for a connection to be made
It makes sense
It stirs creativity

If you need drugs to do this
Pity poor, weak you
So rigid, fenced in, and unimaginative
You must rely on an outside source
To engage in child-like freeform thinking

DEVICE FOR FLIRTATION

You can take the street level view of a third story window
Lights silhouetting figures against the curtains
And you can take the astronomers
With their research studies on different color stars
You can take your victimless crimes and passionate myopia
You can take your currency conversion rates and worthless money
Hand knitted undergarments and airborne viruses

Spin it into a tale of a very ordinary girl
Who practiced self-doubt in a daily workout routine
And cuddled on the couch with the nothingness team

Sculpt it into blaring, deafening chronicles of youth
And middle-aged men who spill their guts
In seaside resorts and watercolor landscapes

The end result is the master conversationalist's completion of training
The loser uses public transportation to get home
The master conversationalist's eyes light up as the room fills his senses and
        he finds a target
"Hello, you must be very tired because you've been running around in my
        mind all day!"

I KILLED A DRIFTER

On the list entitled
"Things that shouldn't be mentioned in your diary"
I killed a drifter

I did it with my bare hands
Full stop
Life contrasting negatively
The manufacturers of timidity
Vs. an inner rage that boils

I killed a drifter
He asked me for a couple of bucks
And barred my way when I tried to walk past him

I did not fear punishment
I'm dangling from a hook
At some point, I stepped off the path
And was never able to find it again

PHARAOH COMPARISONS

Wordproud, at the apex of the pyramid
You wanted us to believe that we were in slavery

Highnose with a foot or hand offered to a loyal subject for kissing
Still desperately searching for the one who will handfeed you grapes

Dusty, defiant, knives out
Roads and temples will never be built this way
Ancient ways fall and disintegrate like the Sphinx's nose
Teeth gnashed, bodies in seizure
Restrained and bound until the right savior can be found

Tent protector,
Why do you live outside the county?

Tent protector,
We need you as counterbalance to the ego's downtown office

FOR ST

Today, I learned to love arrows
Because all you gave me were arrows
An apple on my head….No blindfold!

Yesterday, I went hungry
Because you didn't fill me with anything
Starved at home under the quiet net of night

What does it all mean?
We are always busy as bees
Tomorrow, I will shake the hive
Hoping to feel your sting

ON READING OSWALD SPENGLER FOR THE FIRST TIME

The place in my mind where ideas are formed
Sent spinning as if by gale force winds
Catch me in stiff and rigid poses
Where one idea has to directly negate the other
I know now the inorganic moves like the organic
I know now the lifecycle of a civilization
The birth and golden eras of innovation and invention
The splintering and death due to bloated overextension and decadence
How the popular culture can measure a society's downfall
Fruity prose turns history into a living thing
And the patterns of humanity are revealed as both conscious and
        unconscious

NO NEED TO BUY APPLES

No need to buy apples….We're well stocked here!
I keep thinking of things to do
but everything's been done!
No errands to run
Each entry on life's "to do" list already ticked off

If I could see the blood in my veins x-ray style
I would notice it slowing down from a rush, a flood to a steady hum
The horizon is limited
The scope of vision is limited
Ambition's been baked into a pie and served in small, easy to eat slices
It is an apple pie of course

PLANET SEXY

Loneliness is a sign taped to my back
Kick me, I'm freaky
Kick me, I'm not freaky enough
This has led me to volunteer for the program
Ahhhh when's the spaceship coming?

An orbiting body turned on its dark side
Gravity plus infatuation minus the booster rockets
Used to think I was just miserable
When all along I was an astronaut
Circling the galaxy inside my head
I can only stomach a world very different from this one
I won't survive re-entry

I WANT TO BE ON GOOD TERMS

Finally finding a way to bridge the gap
Between all I disdain and all I need
The compromise is maturity

I want to be on good terms
With the roaring of my heart
And the rhythm of the sea
And feeding and clothing myself
And the underbelly masses suffering through lives of suicide

My lifelong friend, you no longer need to protect me
From the love criminals stomping through the streets
My lifelong friend, this is what open eyes see

Older couples who still make love
$3.50 lunches at the paradise bar and restaurant
Selfless acts from lifelong spinsters
Renew my faith in life

I want to be on good terms
So, my lifelong friend, you can let me go
Don't be scared
There will still be enough of me left
My personality, you won't be alone

CHILD MOLESTER SANTA'S

I know something's not right with Christmas
All I think about is all I can acquire
I know something's not right with capitalism
Brand loyalty starts in infancy
And it's abuse when they fill your head with pretty things
Pushing out the burgeoning quest for knowledge

They warped your mind
Not with alcohol on their breath and late night visits to your bedroom
But with marketing plans aimed at children
Sit on my lap, little girl
And let me tell you how we are all exploited

14x50

Two sides to an argument
One is so much more well-defined than the other
One has much more support than the other

If the jungle is unreal
Do I still need to beat a path?
If the strawman is a hollow threat
Why do the crows still take flight?

The merits of the debate
Do not include a provision for evidence
And raw unvarnished truth blurted out in the heat of battle

If the length is ten times greater or more than the width
And someone interrupts with a point of order
Will the underdogs be brave enough to take a direct question?

THE RITUAL OF BEING INSIDE

Cornered at last by a new language
A new set of ideas
A trade and barter system
I must learn this new form of governance

When doors close on fingers
And new doors fail to open up
One must know the exact etiquette
In order not to find someone's weapon in your back

And when I'm finally released
My skin greets the sunlight with an unhealthy gray pallor
My teeth are rotten and unable to bite down on old freedom
My eyes are painful and sensitive to light

Let's judge the crime
By the society the criminal acts out against
When we acted out against the wrongs committed against the heart
In jest, they threw away the key
I'll take a drink, exercise, any form of escape
But always end up in solitary

THE LOVE THAT WILL KILL YOU

This will be the last time
You take an object directly to heart
And this object is just a space filler
A replacement that can't be bought

This will be the last time
Your blood turns cold and feet are unable to move
A babbling, drooling fool with nothing better to do

This will be the last time
Cupid slew monstrous indecision
Forcing the first few words out
Like a victim of choking receiving a blow to the solar plexus

There is a bond that forms
With something potentially fatal
It covers your face and hands with warm, rotten kisses
When you reach a point where you want to break away,
It's too late for that!

Over our heads then buried under six feet of soil
To find what makes a man/woman complete
Is to find finality
Finality of life!, an addict's dream!, the hollow person's burning needs
    snuffed out!

LIKE A HUSBAND FROM THE LOWER CLASSES

Unburden myself to a plastic wife
That no one would have ever thought to talk to
I don't need your permission to live my life
I've got my hands on a beautiful trophy
Face value, no abstractions
And I don't care about how many men have been inside
As long as I'm the one whose name is on the front door

Rooms in which to store priceless things
Appraised and insured, shown to people you could care less about
She is shown to people you could care less about
The view from below the poverty line is all about achieving face value
It's ugly, it's frantic
I think I would rather be alone the rest of my life

A FRIEND OF BEAUTY

We were soldiers still wearing the clothes of battle
We were only moving forward through the empowerment of weary triumph
Too tired to resist the orders for further killing and Christmas gifts
I saw something dazzling and switched to second person

You were colorful like the banana split men
You were presumptuous like the cocky not yet announced winner
You were miraculous like the once in a lifetime universal anomaly
You've seen people change their lives for the best and for the worst
And you've accepted your own limitations

Cuckolded by the destiny that didn't wait
Enjoyed itself with whatever was available
There is no more devastating form of anarchy
A different type of battlefield awaits us comrades

THE TRUTH WILL HARM YOU

Made not right
By truth and
It's more than "you're ugly and boring etc."
It's a full scale betrayal of a birthright as a human being

Surely we can treat each other better than this
Mr. Sugarcoating with his fingers hooked into quotations
Or the waiter who looks like Joseph Stalin
His striking features….If I was an artist, I would draw him

Bulldozed and pummeled
By truth and
An orthodoxy that knows no higher power
And a glimmer of hope in the eye of deceit

Girlfriendly outsiders taking the lion's share of greetings
She sends me no text message or e-mail
Who makes the violence? Who creates the violators?
Unpleasant things are always explained as being for our own good

Spit upon, kicked, and deeply ignored
By truth and
The up in nowhere to go but up
Is the start of a voyage beyond immortality's reign

THE ORPHANS

The orphans don't have a monopoly in being unclaimed
They are not the only ones without a framework in which to wrap growing
    up around
Springing from a fountain that had not received a coin
Having a family can be worse than not having a family

In a nighttime of childhood,
Where a blue light softly invades the darkness by the door
In the hour of the early morning only good for unsettled, disturbed
    thoughts
A quaint sentimentality is not something to fall back on
Instead, tender self-defeat is the bed ridden rat-eared dogma of family

They tried to have a fun fair to cheer up the orphans and to raise money
Tickets were ten dollars each
Let's hold hands and feel uncomfortable
The charitable run out of things to say to society's bottom rung

HEAVY LEGS

Our story is to be continued
Our infinite has no boundaries
Even though you crush me a lot
Even though you crush me without meaning to

The disused physiology packs more and more upon its frame
With a statue's inscrutable allure to a worshipper
Pincers pinch to accompany crab like teasing

Our time of familiarity knows no end
Your ample frame represent the healthy cycle of life
You are big in the hips, roomy
Even though you crush me in the gentlest way possible
Even though you crush all possibilities with an absence of malice

MIDNIGHT AT THE WAX MUSEUM

I feel adverse at unwarranted public displays of affection
As well as every emotion held in check
Just waiting to find the middle ground between the two extremes

The devil could not ensure a phonier grimace
Someone talks into a cell phone that's not even turned on
To get attention

It's midnight at the wax museum
The exhibits come to life and make a form of conversation
The bare bones – no feeling or interest in another life form

I come to life on a dare from Jack the Ripper
I come to life to find there is no there there
Your bondage slaves are waiting to be freed
I am the observer of sentience used unwisely

DIVINE LIFE ORGANIZATION

What is the purpose of this organization?
This is a question I have asked before
I am hungry for anything
Waiting for something to push my mind around
Windmilling
They were very patient
And didn't allow me to wear shoes indoors

What is the purpose of this organization?
My question was still unanswered
Divine rites of spiritual passage
Preparing the body, the mind long since departed
Free food afterwards
Simple and wholesome
Rice with nuts in it, watery tea

HUMPTY DUMPTY BETRAYAL

You painted it and you pointed it out
And are familiar with the arrivals and departures
Teamwork frees a member from pre-existing arrangements
A suit worn loosely over skin and bone

You made a travesty and you tore open the envelope
And are noxious like the fumes of an older model car
You act on your own but try to pretend you are one of the gang
Sweaty palms prove the guilt of this attempted association

You tore open your stomach and you scattered your vital organs
Realtime frenzy from a man pushed to the limit
The team didn't support you and never visited you during your stay
They can still stitch you up like one of these dolls young girls beat the hell
    out of

FRIENDS OF YOUR OWN AGE

Curtis was a friend of mine
Curtis was the end of mine
We don't have new friends after the age of 35

I'm not going out and meeting people
I'm not taking names
Is it true we don't have new friends after the age of 35?

You are a dad
Perhaps driven mad
By the loss of freedom in your lifestyle

Before the age of 35,
I wore the skin of a slain animal
But was still not accepted as a part of the tribe

MONEYSTOMACH

The luck of the insatiable hedonist
Coming from the Eden with a hole in it
Patting a statue's swollen belly hoping this luck will rub off
Lighting candles, chanting for the promise of cash
The wanton appetite that can never be satisfied
Inspiring rituals conducted by others who want the same
No prayers for flood victims or starving children
They rub their tired eyes and testify to their working existence

In the shadow of the factory,
Too busy to think of another way to live life
Too busy with the mortgage
Too busy with groceries

An existential crisis is a luxury
My minds pre-occupied just trying to survive

FIVE DIFFERENT TYPES OF FREE EXPRESSION FIGHTING TO BE FIRST THROUGH THE EXIT

The inventor of the first working time machine
Disprover of Genesis
Didn't dare to think in a linear structure
Tantamount to the mind's breakthrough compared with magic

Magic? Synapses firing squad "Ready….Aim"
People process information differently
Are you a kinesthetic learner?
The kind who gets something down by creating it with their hands

I only know 1/5 of what you're thinking
I only know about paying the consequences for someone else's bad behavior
Diverts the personality down different doorways
Splintering now splintered
Each piece has a different story to tell

THE COLDEST DAY OF THE YEAR

Baby let me follow you down
Into the world of self-inflicted hurt
Take me to the place where they have accidents
That are not seen as unavoidable

Let the waters rush back to fill the gap
Let the crowd disperse, the show is over
Creaking and groaning heart sputters and comes to a complete standstill

I'm disconnecting from a life that's lived before
Lost on an eternal glacial pathway
Falling asleep in zero degree weather
This is when angels kiss blue lips
And all this happened since man opened the word
On the coldest day of the year

THE PEOPLE WHO KNOW DEATH

Sitting in the doctor's office
Waiting for my appointment with the machine
The woman behind the front desk asks my date of birth
All the employees are friendlier than what is normal in this part of town
Want to know where I'm from and what I do

But their politeness masks a pity
Both natural and rehearsed, part of the job and part of any decent person's character
They know the effects of the worst type of news because they see it every day

And although I left this medical establishment
With a giddy heart and a sense of relief
And the woman at the front desk was more professional and less warm on the way out
I do feel I dodged a bullet
Something large and black and growing in my brain
Which made me dizzy and unwell

The knowledge of death
Is gained from seeing it on someone's face
While they are still alive
I am free from that for now
But we are always under mortality's shadow

www.ingramcontent.com/pod-product-compliance
Lightning Source LLC
Chambersburg PA
CBHW021023090426
42738CB00007B/882